From D.I.V.A. to Disabled

A Determined Individual with a Victorious Attitude

Diary of a D.I.V.A.

Dr. Michelle King-Huger

ISBN 978-1-64492-078-7 (paperback)
ISBN 978-1-64569-142-6 (hardcover)
ISBN 978-1-64492-079-4 (digital)

Christian Faith Publishing, Inc.
832 Park Avenue
Meadville, PA 16335
www.christianfaithpublishing.com

Printed in the United States of America

Dedication

For my dearly departed husband, Anthony Jerome Huger, a.k.a. "Tony," may he rest in peace.

Contents

Acknowledgments

This diary is written in special recognition and love for my son, Jerome W.E. Huger, and my mother, Willie Mae King. My brothers, Woodie Geoffrey and Michael Lee, and for all of my family and friends. My father Woodie King Jr., and my aunt Sandra. For all of the d.i.v.a.s around the world who I do not know. Especially for the d.i.v.a.s I know and love, and many who have passed on.

Opening statement for Diary of a D.I.V.A.: Another year and I am still here, 2019!

From the writings of "Determined Individual with a Victorious Attitude!"

Life is a never-ending journey. I started my writing in 2014 and through a series of flare-ups with my condition; it took me a while to get back on track. However, with support, continuous prayer, and a loving family I am ready to publish! My target audience is wide ranging. Anyone who is going through similar circumstances, those who care for those in need, as well as people who work in the therapeutic and medical fields who reach thousands of individuals on a continuous basis hopefully will find my writing useful. I hope that my writing can also be useful to those teachers and administrators instructing people who desire to go into nursing as a profession. I want my writing to be an inspiration to many.

Well, let us see what has changed since my last entry in 2016. Many of our loved ones are no longer with us and many of our loved ones have brought new life into this world. The circle of life is a continuum. Elections of 2016 have different individuals in the White House, Congress, and Senate. There have been horrific events, both natural and those caused by man, through-out the world and in our country. Millions of dollars are still being spent on war and strategic military defense, and less on medical care and cures. There are many more cuts for insurance coverage for the millions of Americans who suffer with debil-itating diseases.

Remember that we are all here for a reason and seasons. What is your purpose? Can you become an agent of change?

Entry 1
Prologue/Introduction

Would you or others characterize you as a D.I.V.A.—a Determined Individual with a Victorious Attitude? My diary of inspiration was written especially for people who can say that they have lived their lives as independent, educated, loving and productive members of society. D.i.v.a.s, whose life has been curtailed by a chronic illness that has given them a disability that has changed their lives forever. They have now joined an exclusive club where member-ship is free. Some of us are given our membership status because of one or many of the multitudes of illnesses that afflict human beings daily. Some have debilitating strokes which can cause paralysis. Others are born with sickle-cell anemia, diabetes, or one or more than one of the big 'C's, which are so numerous that I will only list a few. Some examples are prostate, colon, ovarian, breast, lung, or kidney cancer. Many individuals are suffering from leukemia, kidney failure, multiple sclerosis, Parkinson's, bone marrow, or Lou Gehrig disease/ALS.

Let us not forget the d.i.v.a.s that have children born with cerebral palsy and many cancers and illnesses and they are given membership status into this club as well. Some d.i.v.a.s that have been included due to unfortunate accidents that have contributed to their disability have been allowed membership status into this exclusive club as well. The list is so long that it bears heavy on my soul.

Entry 2
Membership is Free

What disturbs me the most is that there are no known cures for so many of the debilitating illnesses that have been around for centuries. Medicine and physical therapy seems to be the only response given by those in the medical profession. Investigative research and billions of dollars have been spent on the study of these chronic illnesses that afflict millions of people and still doctors have no answers or cures since the cure for polio was discovered hundreds of years ago that can be successful with today's illnesses, really! Today we are living in the twenty-first century, where billions of dollars are spent to send men into space, and even more for strategic military warfare.

On September 16, 2014, while watching the NBC nightly news they concurred with my statement and I have higher standards and expectations to resolve medical conditions that affect millions of Americans. However, I feel my concerns continue to fall on deaf ears. Therefore, I will speak to my fellow d.i.v.a.s and warmly welcome you into this exclusive club where membership is free.

Entry 3
Now It's Time

It took me a while to decide to share my thoughts and feelings, but now I feel it is time. I really do not know why this is a good time. Maybe because I don't cry as much, maybe because I've always been told that writing is good for the soul and my soul needs healing.

I hope that I can be an inspiration and help to others.

I have a box of tissues nearby and my crying towel because my tears flow easily. When I go to doctor's offices, therapy sessions, or anywhere and people ask me to tell them when things started to change. When did you notice your disability started to take control? A box of tissues is nearby or my "crying towel" is close which I need for comfort. Every day and each night I praise and thank God, because my praise is continuous. I thank him for waking me up each day and keeping me in my right state of mind. I thank God for showing me that even through it all I must praise him and be grateful. I must keep the faith and believe in his goodness. That even though I'm going through a lot, there are so many others that are facing a disability or a chronic illness that is worse than mine.

> *And hope maketh not ashamed; because the love of God is shed abroad in our hearts by the Holy Ghost which is given unto us. (Romans 5:5)*

Entry 4
The Larva Stage

Yes, I was a D.I.V.A. that is now disabled and I am a member of this exclusive club. I worked in the New York City public school system for thirty years and I strongly believe in excellence in education. I enjoyed my career and I really feel grateful for all of the thousands of lives that I touched daily. I have completed four postgraduate degrees, a Bachelor's in Education, two Master's degrees; one in Education and the other Master's in Administration and Supervision.

After successfully completing the Doctor of Education program, I was a proud recipient of a Doctoral Degree as an Education Specialist in Administrator Leadership. I made a six-figure salary and drove the finest cars like Jaguars and Mercedes, just to name a few. Yes, I know I was a d.i.v.a.!

After completing my degree I was preparing myself to become a professor before I became ill. I had two surgeries within a six-month period in 2011, and during physical therapy, one therapist noticed that I was not healing properly. My doctors thought I was just healing slowly, but the disability was just beginning, it was in the larva stage.

My mother lived near me in New Jersey but it became too cumbersome for her to take care of me from a distance. She decided that it would be easier and healthier for us to live together and we moved into a home she bought in North Carolina. I was still walking with a cane at this time.

We started seeing different doctors in North Carolina with the hope of finding out what was going on with me.

After several x-rays, tests, and MRI exams, I was later diagnosed with progressive MS. Literally progressing from one cane to two, and from a walker to a wheelchair. Crazy, how quickly life can change.

Entry 5
Joining the Ranks

I've joined the ranks of millions of disabled Americans who were once productive and independent members of society who now depend on loved ones and caregivers for so many things. Things that I used to take for granted like getting up daily and getting dressed to go to work are past memories. Now I have difficulty getting in and out of the bed without the assistance of a cane. I no longer have the ability to drive a car, or get in and out of a car without assistance.

Loved ones prepare meals for me and help me get up when I fall. So much I used to take for granted, like the ability to walk with a normal gait, to stand more than three minutes, going to work, cooking, or going outside without someone taking me. Driving, shopping, traveling, and intimacy are just a few of the things that I no longer have as an independent woman. These drastic changes have been a lot for me to bear and sometimes my tears flow easily. It's okay to let your teardrops fall from your eyes like rain drops fall from the sky to help you release your emotions. It is my disability and I will cry if I want to. You would cry too if this happened to you.

> *Thou wilt shew me the path of life: In the presence is fullness of joy; at the right hand and there are pleasures forever more. (Psalm 16:11)*

Entry 6
Memories

Memories can make us happy and keep a smile on our face and in our hearts. Some things that keep you strong and lift your spirits are remembering the good times. We need this when we are going through so much and our burdens are heavy and our shoulders feel weak.

My husband was the love of my life and my best friend. He was the proprietor of a car wash and detailing shop on River Road in Edgewater,

NJ, named "Wash and Shine Plus." He was a true D.I.V.A. who definitely lived life to the fullest. He worked hard and made sure that his family lived well. We drove his and her Jaguars, and he was a wonderful husband and father to our son and his children. He passed away in 2007. When he became ill doctors informed him that he needed to wear a pacemaker, but like so many others when dealing with drastic changes everyone handles their individual illness differently. I'm not sure if he realized that the decision he made not to wear a pacemaker would have such strong effect on those who loved him so very much.

Although he is no longer here with me and with all the people he loved and those who loved him dearly, he has left me with so many good memories that will forever make me smile, especially our son, Jerome W.E. Huger.

Memories of eating at the best restaurants and shopping in the finest stores on the East Coast, and fortunate to shop in some of the best stores on Rodeo Drive in Beverly Hills on the West Coast stay fresh on my mind. Traveling to spas in Scottsdale, Arizona, and beaches of the Turk and Caicos islands are memories that will last my lifetime. Yes, I was truly a D.I.V.A. Many of you can identify with me like the d.i.v.a.s that also lived the best that life could offer, because I saw you in the circle. Some of you have traveled to places that I have only dreamt about and places that I only read about in magazines and novels, like many of my fellow d.i.v.a.s.

There are so many d.i.v.a.s. in the world that I don't know on a personal basis. Some of you I see at doctor's offices, physical therapy, and read about in the newspaper, magazines, or hear about on the news. So many d.i.v.a.s have been affected by a chronic illness or disabilities that changed their lives forever. Statistics give reports about the millions of people in our country and around the world. Whether you have traveled or not, whether you have money or not, it doesn't matter, you still are a d.i.v.a. to my heart because you are child of God. When we think of our friends and loved ones who have an illness or who have passed on I want you to take it one day at a time. Please do not forget to smile and remember the good times.

Entry 7
Medication: A Crutch or Cure

Many people think of medications as a crutch and not a cure for what ails us. Our doctors prescribe medications for pain for our chronic illnesses that are necessary. However, we hear many news reports that pain medications can cause a dependency. Many of us are prescribed the same medications for pain. We sleep a lot and did not feel that much changed in our pain level. Although the medications are needed, I did not want to become dependent on pain medication. I was literally in a difficult situation, between a rock and a hard place.

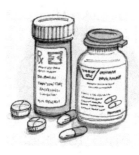

After reading several health books and consulting with my doctors, I decided to lessen my intake of prescribed medications. I decided to eat healthier and increase vitamin supplements. Changing your eating habits is not easy but I was determined not to make medication my crutch. Even with my chronic illness and disability, I want the remainder of my life to be the best and healthiest it could.

> *But in the fruit of the Spirit is love, joy, peace, long-suffering, gentleness, goodness, faith. (Galatians 5:22)*

Through our suffering, we must move forward with determination. We must keep our thoughts positive and not focus on the negative things that have happened in our lives. Release yourself from hurt, release yourself from pain and do not suffer in silence. Meditation and prayer can help make medication a cure and not a crutch.

Your medical physician is also a key component of your well-being, and he or she is part of the cure for our illness and disability. Make sure that you are comfortable with your doctors. It makes all the difference in the world when you are going through such a difficult time. You need to make sure that when you see your doctor you do not leave the office feeling more upset or discouraged than you were when you went in for your appointment. Kind words of compassion about what you are going through means a lot. Having a non-compassionate physician or therapists means a lot and should be avoided at all costs. I have dealt with this situation and I did not return to physicians or physical therapists that were not being considerate of my circumstances. I now have doctors and therapists who are understanding and supportive and they have become an integral part of the cure for my wellness. It makes a world of difference. Many in the medical profession support the use of medicinal marijuana to deal with our pain. Look how times have changed!

No matter how difficult it might be, I want you to try to find humor and laughter in your life. Even if you have to think about things in your past that may be difficult, make every effort to try to smile. Dr. Harvey J. Cohen, a renowned geriatrician, has stated that numerous studies have shown that laughter can reduce stress, improve your immune system, and even release pain. There are many 'laughter clubs' around the globe and many of the participants have chronic illnesses. I agree with Dr. Cohen, like so many others in the medical profession, that laughter is a way of coping and dealing with difficult situations. Make every effort to avoid making medication a crutch, but explore the various ways that they can become a cure for your conditions.

Entry 8
My Crying Towel

My crying towel is nearby when I started to write these next entries, for so many of my fellow d.i.v.a.s that God has called home. I loved my husband dearly, and I loved my friends dearly, and they will always weigh heavy on my mind. As I share my diary of encouragement and inspiration, I want to start by sharing some of my personal suffering with you. There were so many days and nights that my pain was so great and so strong that all I could do was cry, rock, and moan. My mother would come into my room to hug me. She would rub the painful areas and pray for me and with me. I would ask God why was I tormented with such agonizing pain and through the tears and with the pain, my praying is continuous. I would pray and say that I am a child of God and I know that you Lord suffered for me and hear my humble cry. I would rock back and forth while waiting for the medication to subside the pain.

Lord; rebuke me not in thine anger, neither chasten me in thy hot displeasure. Have mercy upon me, O Lord; for I am weak: O Lord, heal me; for my bones are vexed. My soul is also sore vexed; but thou, O Lord, how long? Return, O Lord, deliver my soul: oh save me for thy mercies sake. For in death there is no remembrance of thee: in the grave who shall give thee thanks? I am weary with my groaning; all the night make I my bed to swim; I water my couch with my tears. Mine eye is consumed because of grief; it waxeth old because of all mine enemies. Depart from me, all ye workers of iniquity; for the Lord hath heard the voice of my weep-

ing. The Lord hath heard my supplication; the Lord will receive my prayer. Let all mine enemies be ashamed and sore vexed; let them return and be ashamed suddenly. (Psalm 6:1–10)

I am a living example that prayer is a powerful means of communication, which has helped me and continues to help me tremendously.

Entry 9
How Can I Complain?

I have learned that I must take one day at a time hoping and praying that there will be better days on the horizon. When your body is in pain, and your heart is heavy, and you ask yourself why you are still here, realize there must be a reason. Understand that when your time comes, God will call you home. We are still here for a reason and we must reflect on those we love and who loves us. Are we able to help others no matter how small it may seem? Can the help be that they love you so much and you just need to be around a little longer? I realize that God is all knowing and powerful and when our time comes, God will call you home.

I knew so many of my fellow d.i.v.a.s that have experienced aggressive cancers that went through their bodies like a river flows to the ocean. I loved them and I still do. They will always be on my mind and in my heart because of the memories we shared. However, I now understand that God will not let us handle more than we can bear and when the burden becomes too heavy, and when the pain and suffering becomes too great, God knows.

When I am depressed over my situation God always shows me how someone else is suffering more than I. When the weakness in my legs makes it difficult to move, God then shows me a man with none.

I then asked myself, "How can I complain?" When I look at the news and hear reports about crazed individuals that take the lives of others, I ask myself "How can I complain?" Being like many who suffer from debilitating and dramatic changes in life like health issues, losing loved ones, and financial situations are just some examples of life-changing events and I wanted to write and share my diary with my fellow d.i.v.a.s. I want to offer words of encouragement and support. When I was stricken with this chronic illness, it stopped me in my tracks and the world as I once knew it was no longer the same. I was sinking in quicksand but I refused to drown because I am a survivor.

I refuse to go further in a downward spiral of despair. As author, Alice Walker urges: "When life descends into the pit I must become my own candle willingly burning myself to light up the darkness around me."

Entry 10
Moving Forward

Many people ask me how do I keep such a positive attitude and my life has taken such a three-sixty. You can best believe that I have my bad days, but I am determined to let the good ones outweigh the bad. I will prove to myself that I can and will have more sunny days because life has definitely proven to me that I can stand the rain. I will become victorious in this battle!

I want to share with you the steps that I used to move forward.

Step one: Self-reflection—I took time to reflect on what happened to me and how I must accept and deal with my disability, no matter how much it changed my life. I developed a deeper and stronger spiritual dimension because this helped me to understand how not to focus on my problem and realize others suffer more than I. In addition, I think about how I can help others in any way possible became a new objective. I have given more to charitable organizations and have learned to accept the things that I cannot change.

Step two: Sharing my feelings—I share my feelings and listen to others more than before. I discuss my condition with others and I was surprised to know that many people are going through experiences that I would never have imagined. Communicating with others is key when you are in a dire situation. When someone understands what you are going through and then in turn you can listen to what they are going through makes everyone feel so much better. Little things mean a lot and having a person(s) to share with you lightens the weight on your shoulders.

Step three: Think positive—Maintain a positive attitude! Yes, we all experience depression but I will not allow myself to be swallowed in the quicksand. I think of my life as a transformation of who I have become. I am stronger. I am wiser and more aware of the suffering of others. I am a survivor and I want you to become a survivor too. I have accepted the fact that I am a new member in this exclusive club where membership is free.

I am no longer a part of the working environment and accessibility to social affairs have dwindled to a non-existing state are some of the hardest pills for me to swallow. The lack of intimacy makes me feel like I am less of the woman that I used to be which funnels emotions of anger, sadness, and depression. Maybe I need to purchase some toys for entertainment purposes until I find someone to hold, kiss, and love me unconditionally.

I mentioned previously that my God always shows me someone in a condition that is worse than mine when I'm complaining and whining about myself. One evening, I had the pleasure of viewing a "Fit and Health Discovery" television segment entitled "Paralyzed and Pregnant" in October of 2014, on NBC nightly news. It featured how a woman became a quadriplegic after an accident she suffered while on vacation. Even though after becoming seriously disabled she went online, found love, married, and gave birth to a son. Wow, she truly demonstrated the spirit of a D.I.V.A., a determined individual with a victorious attitude! Once again, I reiterate, how can I complain when she demonstrated so much strength?

Prayer works for me, but I have learned to incorporate the equation of prayer plus faith to equalize action. Until love happens, and even if it does not, I thank God for he has blessed me with a potpourri of wonderful memories that will last my lifetime. I will forge ahead by focusing on my writing ability and literary skills. I will enjoy audiotapes, art, and music. I have joined discussion groups and religious organizations as added ingredients in my action equivalent. Often times I wonder if I will ever meet a man that I shall love again, and will he love me despite my disability, or would this be an impossible dream?

> *For with God nothing shall be impossible. (Luke 1:37)*

Entry 11
Don't Push Me

Please don't push me because I'm living my life close to the edge. When such dramatic changes occurred in my life for a long time I felt like I was existing in a ball of confusion. It became difficult and extremely emotional for me to make rational decisions about my health, and well-being.

Conversations became overwhelming and I cried uncontrollably. When my illness was diagnosed and doctors described the symptoms that would soon become evident with my disability, I battled with feelings of avoidance and depression that became paramount each day. My emotions were tumultuous like the lava that flows from volcanic eruptions. Only fellow members of this exclusive club could possibly understand what I was going through.

> *When God pushes you to the edge, trust Him fully because only two things can happen. Either He will catch you when you fall or He will teach you how to fly. (Unknown)*

It seemed as if I have plenty of time for self-reflection in my present condition. I think about my childhood and how I was raised. My parents loved me and taught me the value of education, demonstrating strength, wisdom, and above all, the love of God. I have learned to never stop trying and to never give up no matter how difficult things might seem. I believe in myself and value the importance of education and I have demonstrated this by having a career for thirty years with the New York City Department of Education. I have successfully completed four postgraduate degrees culminating with the Doctoral degree. My family is very proud of my accomplishments. My praise is continuous!

Finally, how can my self-reflection help me now? I strongly believe my upbringing and life lessons can help me in the war that I am waging against affliction and disability. No matter how hard it gets, I will maintain a positive attitude. This is a key component to a successful strategy in this battle. My faith is strong and I will hold on to God's unchanging hand thus allowing me to make the checkmate move to become a victorious individual in life's constant battle.

I am somebody regardless of my gender, race, status in life, and health. I will always realize how powerful words can be. When I feel overwhelmed with waves of depression and self-pity, I repeat these words "I am somebody." No matter how beautiful a day may be or how bright the sun may shine, I seem to experience more cloudy days than I want. My efforts are steadfast and I must change what many defined as an unattainable goal to my advantage.

Things that used to be insignificant now become something that I appreciate and cherish. That light from the dawn of a new day is cherished. The warmth of the sun on my body allowing vitamin D to become a natural healing proponent for me is appreciated. Yes, at this stage in my life, I recognize things that I used to consider minute now are so very important. When I am sad and lonely

I think of a few of my favorite things and then I don't feel so bad.

My fellow D.I.V.A.s, reflect on some of your favorite things and engulf yourself with them. Literary works, art, inspirational quotes, and my educational accomplishments surround me. I want you to make your immediate surroundings overflowing with things that complete you. Music relaxes me and gives my soul and spirit a wonderful feeling that is unexplainable. It turns my frown upside down, in spite of what I am going through. Many in the medical profession as well as persons servicing the elderly and individuals with illnesses agree that music is a therapeutic form of healing. I can give testimony to this conclusion and I believe that many of you will also concur with the statement. I am somebody and I will not allow what I'm going through to take control of my spirit. I will remember that words are powerful and as long as I believe that words can hurt and heal, I want you to chant these three words when you are feeling down. "I am somebody."

Entry 12
Life Experiences

Understand that self-reflection can bring forth emotions that can be positive and negative, and we must not avoid facing the outcome no matter the results. When people reflect, they analyze and categorize their experiences and hopefully they will learn from them. Facing conditions associated with difficult situations can become a tumultuous experience.

When I reflect on why some individuals handle their circumstances differently, many aspects and factors contribute to this process. When I analyze situations, I rationalize circumstances and the pros and cons thereof. When I categorize I tend to sort by commonalities and properties in the results. One aspect that I have focused on relates to whether or not an individual's personal and past experiences, after being diagnosed with a serious illness, make a difference on how said individual responds to their disability. How do many of us maintain positive attitudes and the spirit of determination regardless of dismal medical feedback? Could it be that an individual's life experiences are so enriching and fruitful that it makes them stronger?

For me, I can personally bear witness to this statement. My days and nights are filled with blissful memories, which propel me with hopes toward an optimistic future. Carefully analyzing my situation, I am determined that I will be the best that I can be through it all. When depression comes, I shake it off. When pain occurs, I bear it. My faith remains strong and I will not give up because I am a survivor. I am a D.i.v.a a determined individual with a victorious attitude!

Entry 13
Endurance

It is difficult for me to believe that I am facing another surgery! So many of us go through more than one surgical procedure in our lifetime and our life lies in the hands of medical experts. When I realized that I needed another procedure, I discussed important details with love ones who support me. My surgery was successful and I thank God and the medical professionals who performed the operation.

The good, the sad, and the embarrassing phases of rehabilitation are rarely talked about, but I will make mention of it in this entry. The healing process in the hospital varies with each individual facility and that experience can be daunting. Having a positive experience depends on the nursing staff and others that are responsible for your care. Researching the background of the hospitals and rehabilitation facilities makes all the difference in the world. I will now discuss the good news because we all like to hear the good news first. After careful background checks, I ended up in a relatively decent facility. My doctors were professional and knowledgeable, and staff members were enthusiastic and helpful. Activities were engaging and appropriate for my healing needs. During my short-term stay for rehabilitation, I was a witness to stages of depression that I will never forget. Patients were reaching stages that were far beyond the facility's capabilities for assistance. Crying and moaning regularly as they thought of days that were long gone. Not responding when they were spoken to as they clutched their doll babies and brushed their hair, constantly repeating the same thing no matter what question they were asked as they rolled through the corridors in their wheelchairs. You may wonder how I know these things. I engaged in conversation with them all as I wheeled down the corridors, those with one leg and others with none. As I said previously, how can I complain?

The embarrassing aspect of rehabilitation, is when you must trust individuals you do not know with your personal care. They see you in your nakedness in the barest of your existence. These individuals cleaned my body as I swallowed my pride and sacrificed my self-esteem to regain my health. I have the deepest respect for the caregivers who showed me kindness at my weakest point. I sincerely thank them because they make this world a better place for those who are disabled in their time of need. The good, the sad, and the embarrassing aspects of living strengthen your resolve in the struggle for improved health.

Entry 14
Transformation

Life is a cycle beginning at the first breath you take and ending with your last. In the interim, I will enjoy each day to the fullest. I will plan for those I leave behind. I will ensure that my living will not be in vain. Maintaining a victorious attitude is very important so with each day and every night there is purpose for your existence. This is my goal and my life objective. I know that I am not a robot. Sometimes I cry hard, but when the going gets tough I know that I must keep going, as we all must. I am determined that my son will have something put away for his future and I am determined to help those less fortunate than myself. I will keep my victorious attitude because I am a true D.I.V.A.—a determined individual with a victorious attitude! This is how I want to be remembered.

Sharing my diary was good for my soul and I hope it was an inspiration to you as well. Being a prayerful person, I want to help others because it helps to make my life worthwhile. Even though life takes us on many journeys, we will realize that we are still here for a reason. Each day hold onto the memories of those you love because it keeps you strong. Remember, memories last a lifetime. Thank all the people who have helped you and the people that continue to help you. Remember that each day above ground is a good day and somebody loves you...especially me. You are a fighter and a survivor and we will not let our disability take our spirit because once that happens there is no reason to open your eyes in the morning.

I will offer some suggestions for my fellow d.i.v.a.s in this exclusive club where the membership is free.

> Share your experiences with others and thank your loved ones and caregivers daily.

> Listen to music because music is uplifting. Look at television or listen to it. Many shows will definitely take your mind off your problems!

> When you leave your home or residence, dress in your neatest and best attire. It will make you feel so much better.

> Surround yourself with beautiful things and that will put a smile on your face.

I have made my final transformation and have emerged from the larva stage to that beautiful black and gold butterfly. Yes, I may be disabled but I am still and always will be a D.I.V.A. But Now I'm a "Determined and

Disabled Individual with a Victorious Attitude!"

So all my fellow d.i.v.a.s tell me, what color is your butterfly?

I am crucified with Christ: nevertheless I live; yet not I; but Christ liveth in me: and the life that I now live I live in the flesh by faith of the Son of God, who loved me, and gave himself for me. (Galatians 2:20)

Sharing tips for caregivers

While reading my October/ November 2015 A.A.R.P. Magazine, I came across some wonderful ideas for caregivers. The month of November is dedicated to the celebration of National Family Caregivers and I would like to share some my favorite random acts of kindness for these wonderful individuals.

- ~ Purchase a low maintenance houseplant
- ~ Take him/her out for a day of relaxation
- ~ Arrange for some special house cleaning in their home

- Arrange for a day spa for some pampering
- Replenish their coffee or tea supply
- Give them a nice bottle of wine
- Hire a geek to help with tech issues
- Send a care/gift package
- Let them know how much you appreciate their time and effort

Reference

A.A.R.P. Magazine, Sharing tips for caregivers, October/November 2015

Anonymous Poem—Entry 8

Cohen, Harvey J. Dr., Renowned Geriatrician, Stay Well Forever, Page 20, August/September 2014, AARP magazine.

Holy Bible—KJV King James Version copyright 2005.

Romans 5:5

Psalm 16:11

Psalm 6:1–10

Galatians 5:22

Galatians 2:20

Luke 1:37

Walker Alice, Author/Poet. Quotation from church bulletin, October 2014, Friendship Missionary Baptist Church.

Color Prints

Microsoft, Window 7. Clip Art

Cover, Butterflies are Free Icon Do, 512(w)x 512(h) pixels, 326 KB, PNG

Caterpillar on Green Leaf Free, 150(w)x 132(h) pixels, 6KB, JPG

Medicine bottles, Windows 7. Clip Art

Addendum

The line was busy.

When you go through an illness, a sudden catastrophe or great pain, my faith allows me to believe that God will call you home. However, I wonder what will happen when the line is busy. We must believe that those in the medical profession and our prayers will see us through. From day to day, we do not know when it will be our last. July 23, 2016 could have been mine.

The line was busy and my God did not call me home. I am staying here for a reason and I will make sure that all of my affairs are in order and my living will not be in vain. I will cross my t's and dot my i's because I have always known how precious life is. Praise God and this D.I.V.A., this black and gold butterfly will never forget to say, "I love you!"

About the Author

Michelle King was born in Detroit, Michigan, on October 1, 1958, and almost died in Charlotte, North Carolina, on July 23, 2016. But, praises to her Lord and Savior, Jesus Christ, the line was busy and she is still here!

Michelle had a happy childhood and moved to New York with her parents at the age of six. Growing up with her mother Willie Mae, an educator, her father Woodie King Jr., a theatrical producer/director, and her two brothers, Woodie Geoffrey and Michael Lee, her house was immersed with the values of education, the arts, and the love of God.

Graduating high school at the age of sixteen, she continued to fulfill her educational pursuits. She received four postgraduate degrees. A Bachelor's in Education, a Masters in Education and a second Masters in Administration and Supervision from C.C.N.Y. After successfully completing sixty plus hours in the Doctor of

Education program she was a proud recipient of a doctoral degree as an Education Specialist in Administrator Leadership. She received her fourth postgraduate degree from Walden Univ.

Michelle strived for excellence in education in her thirty-year career with the New York City Department of Education touching the lives of thousands of children and adults. Dr. Michelle King-Huger received letters of commendation from the Council of the City of New York, the Council of Supervisors and Administrators from the City of New York, and letters of congratulations on retirement and service from President Obama, President Bush, President

Clinton, and President Jimmy Carter acknowledging her rewarding career in education.

She lived in Edgewater, New Jersey and raised her son Jerome until her husband Tony passed away and her health began to decline. She now resides in Charlotte, North Carolina, with her mother who is her primary caregiver.

Dr. Michelle King-Huger who is now disabled wants to inspire others to become agents of change as she warmly welcomes all D.I.V.A.s— "Determined Individuals with a Victorious Attitude" with disabilities—whether they be young or old, rich or poor, of all races and genders as members into this exclusive club where membership is free!